This book is dedicated to Pandy.

Calm Yoga Bear

By Mary Nhin

Illustrated By
Yuliia Zolotova

I have a choice
To be peaceful each **day**.
Staying calm helps me keep
Anxiety and stress **away**.

I get a good night's sleep
Each and every **night**,
And greet each new day
Being thankful for **daylight**.

I climb out of bed
And stretch my arms **tall**,
Reaching high on my tiptoes
So I feel **less small**.

I walk to the corner
And unroll my yoga **mat**.
I start my day with
A Mountain Pose for my **back**.

I swan dive forward
And press my palms **down**.
The stress leaves my eyes
While I listen to nature's **sound**.

I lift half-way up, back flat
With a micro-bend in my **knees**
Breathing in, I gaze past
The cherry blossom **trees**.

And then, I gently jump
Into a Plank **fast**.
I stay low to the ground
For as long as I can **last**.

Next, I move my body forward
And stretch into Cobra, nice and **deep**.
Then, I shift to Downward Dog
With one smooth **sweep**.

I bend my body forward
To a Table Top **pose**.
I feel tension leaving me,
Even in my **nose**.

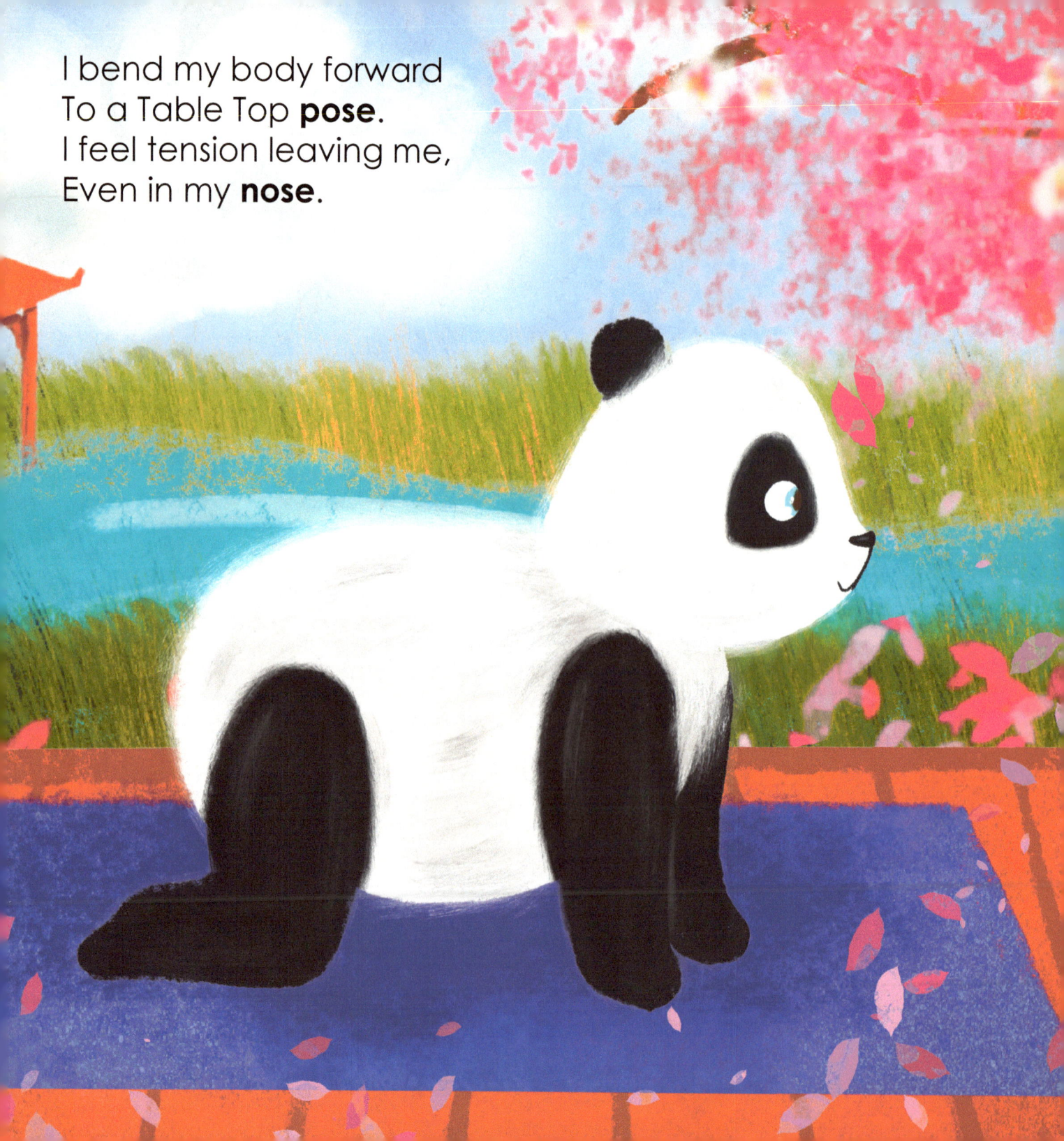

I drop my tummy for Cow pose
As I take a deep **inhale**.
I gaze to the sky
As if I have a **tail**.

Then, I move into Cat pose,
Being mindful of my **breathing**.
I drop my head to exhale
Until I have a good **feeling**.

Next, I sit down for Boat pose
And lift my legs up **high**.
I reach past my knees
And point my toes up to the **sky**.

Then, I move to standing positions.
But first I wiggle each **toe**
Which helps relieve my stress
As I go through my yoga **flow**.

I bend one leg for Tree pose
And balance, standing **tall**.
I'm full of peace and calm,
So I know I'll never **fall**.

Then, I move into Triangle pose
And slide my arm down **low**.
It's a wonderful kind of challenge
To see how low I can **go**.

I finish up with Warrior.
It's my favorite pose to **do**.
And if I feel like extra,
I'll even slip into Warrior **2**.

Then, I lay down for Savasana
To make my body **calm**.
I let my hands go softly,
Feel the air right in my **palm**.

I focus on my breathing,
Deeply in and **out**,
While I rid my mind of
Stress, insecurity, and **doubt**.

I keep my body still
As I open up my **eyes**.
And when I feel I'm ready,
I slowly begin to **rise**.

Rolling up into
A comfortable seated **position**,
Breathing in and out
For my soul's **nutrition**.

Yoga makes me happy
And relieves me of my **stress**.
It's a simple thing I do each day
That leads to much **success**.

Staying calm is a choice
That I like to make each **day**
Because when I'm peaceful
I feel better in every single **way**.

Calm Yoga Bear Sequence Flow

Mountain Pose

- ✓ Improves posture
- ✓ Strengthens thighs, knees, and ankles
- ✓ Firms abdomen and buttocks

Standing Forward Bend
(palms on ground)

- ✓ Strengthens and stretches the legs
- ✓ Gently stretches the hips, thighs, and ankles

Half Standing Forward Bend

✓ Strengthens and stretches the legs
✓ Strengthens the spine
✓ Strengthens the ankles and legs

Plank

✓ Strengthens the arms, wrists, and spine
✓ Tones the abdomen

Cobra

✓ Strengthens the spine
✓ Stretches chest and lungs, shoulders, and abdomen
✓ Firms the buttocks

Downward Dog

✓ Calms the brain and helps relieve stress and mild depression
✓ Energizes the body

Table Top

- ✓ Improves posture
- ✓ Strengthens thighs, knees, and ankles
- ✓ Firms abdomen and buttocks

Cow

- ✓ Stretches the front torso and neck
- ✓ Provides a gentle massage to the spine and belly organs

Cat

✓ Stretches the back torso and neck
✓ Provides a gentle massage to the spine and belly organs

Boat

✓ Strengthens the abdomen, hip flexors, and spine
✓ Stimulates the kidneys, thyroid and prostate glands, and intestines
✓ Helps relieve stress

Tree

✓ Improves balance
✓ Lifted Leg: gently stretches your inner thigh and front of thigh (quadriceps) while strengthening your outer thigh and buttocks (gluteals)

Triangle

✓ Strengthens and stretches the legs and ankles
✓ Stretches the groins, chest and lungs, shoulders
✓ Stimulates abdominal organs

Warrior

- ✓ Stretches the chest and lungs, shoulders and neck, belly, groins (psoas)
- ✓ Strengthens the shoulders and arms, and the muscles of the back

Warrior 2

- ✓ Strengthens and stretches the legs and ankles
- ✓ Stretches the groins, chest and lungs, shoulders
- ✓ Stimulates abdominal organs

Sleeping

✓ Calms the brain and helps relieve stress and mild depression

✓ Relaxes the body

✓ Reduces headache, fatigue, and insomnia

Sitting

✓ Increases balance and core strength.

✓ Calms the mind

www.ingramcontent.com/pod-product-compliance
Lightning Source LLC
Chambersburg PA
CBHW042023090426
42811CB00016B/1719